DISCARD

D is for Down Under

An Australia Alphabet

Written by Devin Scillian and Illustrated by Geoff Cook

To the Flynns—
Chris, Kathy, Kelsey, and Victor
Devin

For Sue—
my wife and buddy
Geoff

Text Copyright © 2010 Devin Scillian
Illustration Copyright © 2010 Geoff Cook

Sleeping Bear Press™
315 E. Eisenhower Parkway, Ste. 200
Ann Arbor, MI 48108
www.sleepingbearpress.com

© 2010 Sleeping Bear Press is an imprint of Gale, a part of Cengage Learning.

First Edition

10 9 8 7 6 5 4 3 2 1

Printed by China Translation & Printing Services Limited, Guangdong
Province, China. 1st printing. 05/2010

Library of Congress Cataloging-in-Publication Data

Scillian, Devin.
D is for down under : an Australia alphabet / written by Devin Scillian; illustrated by Geoff Cook.
p. cm.
ISBN 978-1-58536-445-9
1. Australia—Juvenile literature. 2. Alphabet books. I. Cook, Geoff, 1945-
II. Title.
DU96.S33 2010
994—dc22
2010010738

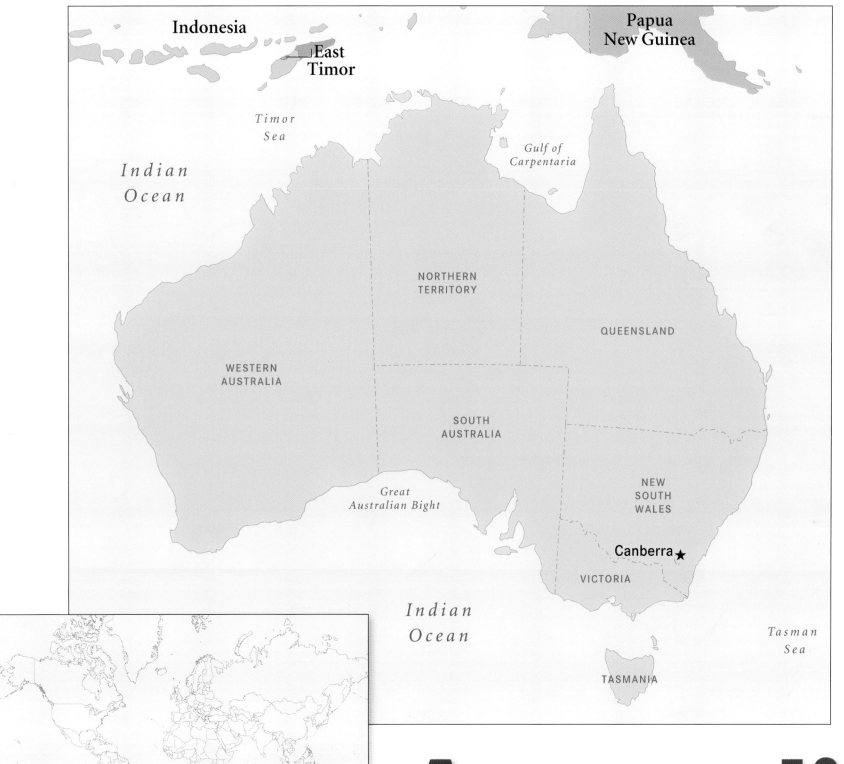

Indonesia

East
Timor

*Timor
Sea*

*Indian
Ocean*

Papua
New Guinea

*Gulf of
Carpentaria*

NORTHERN
TERRITORY

QUEENSLAND

WESTERN
AUSTRALIA

SOUTH
AUSTRALIA

NEW
SOUTH
WALES

*Great
Australian Bight*

Canberra ★

VICTORIA

*Indian
Ocean*

*Tasman
Sea*

TASMANIA

Australia

A a

The Aboriginal people are the natives of the Australian continent. Their culture is among the very oldest on earth, stretching back perhaps 40,000 years. Their traditions are defined by a deep reverence for the natural world around them. Rocks, trees, rivers, canyons—they are all sacred and connected in Aboriginal thought. Through these beliefs, the Aboriginal people learned long ago to live in harmony with their natural surroundings, moving with the seasons to find food and shelter.

The arrival of European settlers in the 1800s had a devastating impact on the Aboriginal people. The settlers brought with them diseases, guns, and a desire for land and resources that overwhelmed the native population. Eventually, British rulers forced the Aboriginal people to abandon their culture and beliefs. At the start of European settlement, nearly 300 native languages were spoken in Australia; today, all but about 20 have largely vanished. But with the passage of time, modern Australians have gained a new respect and understanding for Aboriginal culture, traditions, art, and music. Today's Australia has learned to celebrate the rich and unique nature of its native people.

We'd best begin our trip with a big Australian A
for the Aboriginal people we'll meet along the way.
Long ago they understood in dreams by and by
the spirit of Australia is in the land and sky.

Being the world's largest island, Australia is, of course, surrounded by water. To the east lies the Pacific Ocean; to the west, the Indian Ocean. The northern coast of Australia includes the Timor, Arafura, and Coral Seas. And along the southern coast you'll find the Southern Ocean and Tasman Sea.

There are more than 22,000 miles of beaches on the Australian continent. Most Australians live near the coastal areas of the country—in fact, 85% of the population lives within an hour's drive of the coastline. That means the beach is deeply ingrained in Australian culture.

Australian beaches are extremely diverse, from quiet, crystal-clear pools of water to roaring swells of pounding surf where the world's best surfers gather to challenge enormous waves. Among the most famous beaches are Bondi and Manly in Sydney, St. Kilda in Melbourne, and Cottesloe in Perth.

B is for the beaches, the best you've ever seen.
From Brisbane to Bondi, beyond and between,
Basking in the sunshine or bobbing in the bay,
being barefoot on the beach is a perfect Aussie day.

Australia's crocodiles are found in the state of Queensland in the tropical north. There are two kinds of crocodiles native to Australia. The Johnston's crocodile is found in the freshwater areas of Queensland, while the estuarine crocodile prefers saltwater. Saltwater crocs can grow to be very large and occasionally attack horses and cattle at watering holes.

Several famous Australians have been associated with crocodiles, and thus, many people the world over think of the enormous reptiles when they think about Australia.

Steve Irwin was known as the Crocodile Hunter, and his television adventures in the Australian wilderness taught people everywhere about Australian wildlife.

In 1986 Paul Hogan starred in *Crocodile Dundee*, a movie about a heroic outdoorsman from the Australian Outback. The film introduced many people to Australian culture and language, and Hogan became a kind of Australian ambassador to the world.

Our C is in the water with a very crooked smile.
Don't come any closer; **C** is for crocodile!
He sneaks along in silence, looking for his food.
He has a rotten temper and a nasty attitude.

For letter D, some music please. We'll play a song or two.
A sound like none you've ever heard—**D** is for didgeridoo.
A didgeridoo hums deep and low, a quirky kind of buzz.
Nothing else can make the sound an Aussie didgeridoo does.

The didgeridoo (didj·er·i·doo) is commonly considered the world's oldest wind instrument. Wall paintings in Northern Australia suggest that the didgeridoo has been around for nearly 1,500 years. While the word *didgeridoo* may sound like an exotic Aboriginal term, it's believed to have been a Western term invented to describe the odd-sounding instrument that no doubt seemed so foreign to European settlers. Among Australia's indigenous people there are many different words for a didgeridoo including *yirdaki*, *garnbak*, and *paampu*.

Didgeridoos are made from the thin trunks of live eucalyptus trees that have been hollowed out by termites. They can vary greatly in size from three feet to nearly ten feet long, and they are often intricately decorated.

A didgeridoo makes a long, droning, vibrating sound. While it can be played as a solo instrument for fun, it is also often played in important Aboriginal ceremonies.

D is also for "down under." Most of the world's population sees Australia and New Zealand sitting in the Southern Hemisphere, toward the bottom of the globe. For this reason, both countries are referred to as "the land down under."

Dd

E is for echidna

Here comes our E in shades of brown and yellow.
He's a ball of thorny bristles, a prickly little fellow.
E is for echidna, licking at a termite mound.
He rolls into a spiny ball when trouble comes around.

The echidna is also known as the spiny anteater, and like the anteater, echidnas eat ants and termites. They have powerful claws that they use to tear open rotted logs or anthills in search of their next meal.

The echidna and the platypus are the only animals in a unique class of mammals known as *monotremes*. Monotremes lay eggs like a duck, but raise their young in a pouch like a kangaroo. (The echidna and the platypus are the only mammals that lay eggs.)

Baby echidnas are known as *puggles*, and they live in their mother's pouch until they begin to grow their sharp spines. Echidnas are considered to be very smart, and they've been seen using their spines and snouts to scale steep surfaces like a rock climber.

Echidnas are found only in Australia, New Zealand, and New Guinea.

F f

F stands for freedom; for this great land is free.
It's more than an idea; it's the Aussie pedigree.
The nation of Australia was a prison at the start.
So freedom's forever cherished in the Aussie mind and heart.

For centuries, only the Aboriginal people roamed the Australian continent. But the era of European sea exploration eventually reached "the land down under." The first explorers to reach Australia were likely Dutch. (In fact, for nearly two centuries, the land was known as "New Holland.") It was the British who longed to colonize the world's smallest continent. And since crime had become an enormous problem in England in the late 1700s, an isolated land far away seemed like a good place to send unwanted criminals. The last shipment of convicts arrived in Australia in 1868.

Eventually, a modern Australia was created with six states: New South Wales, Queensland, West Australia, South Australia, the Northern Territory, and Victoria.

Since Australians want to move ahead, their coat of arms, tellingly, includes a kangaroo and an emu in part because they are two animals unable to walk backward. Today Australians occasionally poke fun at their country's origin, but they also believe it gives them a unique understanding of the importance of freedom.

You're swimming around in a snorkel and mask, staring in disbelief, surrounded by our letter G, the Great Barrier Reef. Sharks and starfish, turtles and whales, fish of every size. The colors of the rainbow parade before your eyes.

Considered one of the world's "Seven Natural Wonders," the Great Barrier Reef is the largest coral reef system on earth. It is located along the coast of northeastern Australia in the Coral Sea.

While it is referred to as a single reef, it is actually comprised of nearly 3,000 reefs and 900 islands, stretching about 1,250 miles in length. It is even visible from outer space.

A coral reef is a hub of sea life. Researchers have found about 1,500 different species of fish on the Great Barrier Reef, and new ones are identified each year.

Along with all those fish, the reef is home to 30 species of whales, 6 kinds of sea turtles, and 125 species of sharks and stingrays.

Divers come from all over the world to swim near the endless variety of wildlife. But the ecosystem of the Great Barrier Reef is delicate, and scientists and conservationists work diligently to balance the demands of tourism with the health of the reef.

Gg

H stands for harbor, and one heck of a view.
Welcome to Sydney, sparkling like new.
Climb the Harbor Bridge; look down when you're done.
You'll find the famous Opera House soaring in the sun.

Sydney is the largest city in Australia. Its harbor is considered one of the most picturesque places in the world. On sunny Sydney days, the waters of the harbor are filled with sailboats, cruise ships, ferries, and cargo vessels from all over the world.

The Sydney Harbor Bridge was opened in 1932 and has been a great source of national pride ever since. Cars, trucks, trains, and people all pass across the bridge. Since 1998, thrill-seeking tourists have been allowed to climb the southern half of the bridge. Outfitted in a special suit and attached to the bridge by a wire lifeline, climbers are led by tour guides on a three-and-a-half hour climb to the top. From there they have an incredible view of the Sydney Opera House.

The spectacular Sydney Opera House is an unmistakable symbol of Australia and one of the most recognizable buildings on earth. Designed by Danish architect Jørn Utzon, the Opera House appears to set sail without ever leaving the harbor. While the roofs of the Opera House appear to be a smooth, uniform white, they are actually composed of more than a million white tiles made in Sweden.

But the Sydney Opera House is much more than a building to see. Inside are several theaters that host ballets, operas, plays, and symphonies.

For many years geography experts have debated whether Australia should be considered a continent or an island. On the one hand, Australia is an enormous landmass with plants and animals not found anywhere else in the world (everything from kangaroos to wombats to blue-tongued lizards). On the other hand, it is completely surrounded by water and is occupied by only one nation. So which is it? Is Australia the world's smallest continent or the world's largest island?

Comparisons are often made to Greenland, which is considered an island rather than a continent. But there are a number of differences. The continental plates beneath the ocean suggest that Australia is independent of other landmasses, while Greenland appears to be connected to North America. While there are many unique species in Australia, the plants and animals of Greenland are found elsewhere. There is also such diversity in the Australian landscape, from tropical rainforest to bone-dry desert.

Australians are mixed in their opinions about the island/continent debate. But in what seems to be a wise compromise, Australia is often referred to as "the island continent."

I stands for island, but one that's not too small.
This island is enormous. Just try to see it all!
There's no place else quite like it; that is clearly true.
Australia is a continent, but it's an island, too.

Ii

Australia is home to enormous ranches known as "stations." The young apprentices who work there rounding up sheep or cattle are known as *jackaroos* (for young men) and *jillaroos* (for young women). The massive size of many of the stations means jackaroos and jillaroos have to cover long distances to keep their livestock together. Some modern jackaroos use motorcycles, all-terrain vehicles, and even helicopters to move the herds. But more station hands are returning to horses, a link to tradition and to the fact that horses are not as stressful on the sheep or cattle as the sound of modern machinery.

Some of the finest wool in the world comes from Australian sheep. Once a year (usually in spring), the thick woolen coats of the sheep are removed and turned into wool yarn. In the traditional manner, the sheep are taken to a shearing shed where teams of shearers clip away their thick coats. The clean-shaven sheep then run off to start growing a brand-new coat of wool.

It'll be quite a job, our letter J.
You'll be tending sheep on a long, hot day.
You'll raise them up and shear them, too.
For that's the job of a jackaroo!

Jj

With its position in the Southern Hemisphere, far from most of the world's population, Australia can be difficult to reach. But that isolation also means that animal species were able to develop in Australia and the South Pacific that can't be found anywhere else. Some of these animals have become symbols of Australia.

The kookaburra is a large bird known for its loud call, which sounds very much like human laughter.

Kangaroos are the only large animals that hop to travel. They are *marsupials*, which means mothers raise their young (called *joeys*) in their pouches.

The koala has long been referred to as a koala "bear," but it isn't really a bear at all. Like kangaroos, koalas are marsupials. They live in eucalyptus forests and can survive eating only eucalyptus leaves.

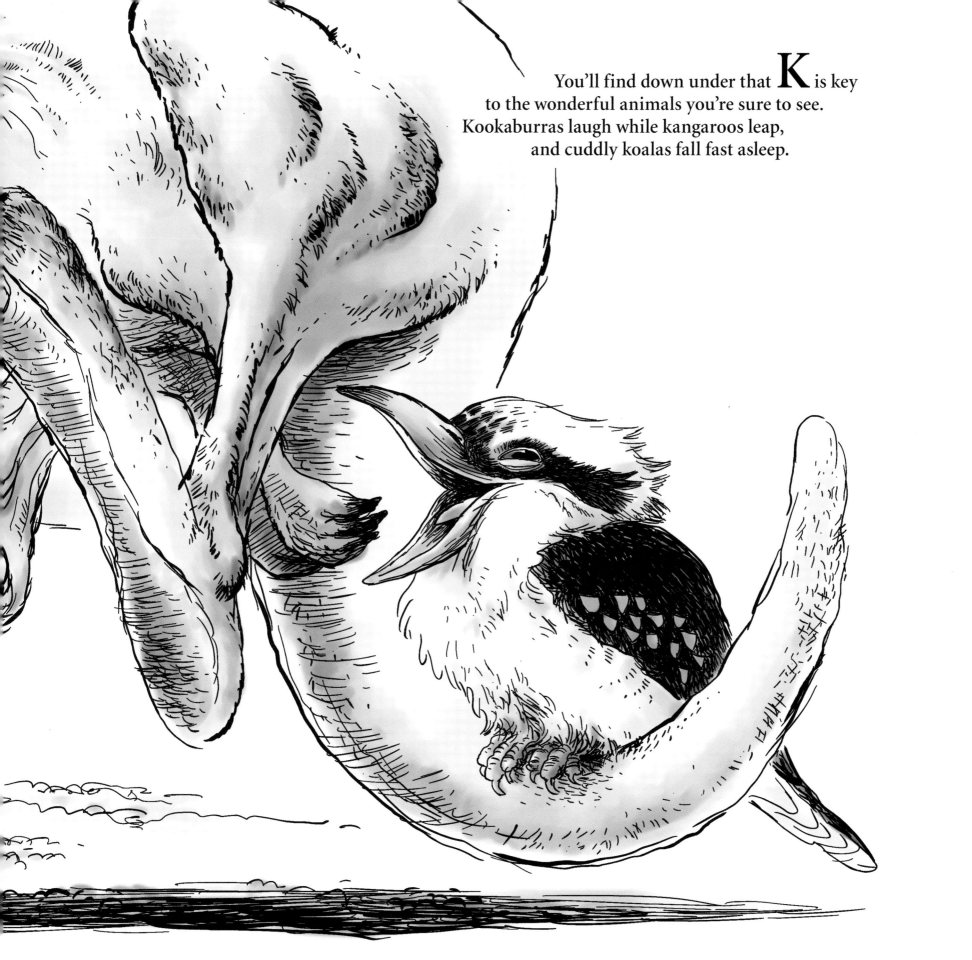

You'll find down under that K is key
to the wonderful animals you're sure to see.
Kookaburras laugh while kangaroos leap,
and cuddly koalas fall fast asleep.

In a land of many beaches, we'll need a watchful eye,
someone to keep us safe when the roaring tide is high.
L is for lifeguard, watching the conditions.
They try to prove their skills in thrilling competitions.

The lifeguard has long been a key figure on Aussie beaches. Thousands of trained volunteer lifesavers patrol the sand and surf, peering into the waves for signs of trouble. The famous Australian beaches are beautiful, but they can also be treacherous. Roaring tides and currents can surprise even experienced swimmers. Surfers who like to be challenged by huge waves can find themselves suddenly swept into dangerous waters.

There are also a number of sea creatures to avoid; a sting from a box jellyfish is not only painful but very dangerous. While shark attacks are rare, it helps if someone is looking out for their telltale fins. Swimmers are advised to swim only at beaches that have trained lifeguards on duty. It's estimated that Australian lifeguards make up to 10,000 rescues a year.

Whether it's swimming in choppy surf, throwing a life preserver to a tired swimmer, or rowing a boat into violent waves, a lifeguard may have to call on a wide array of skills to save someone. At "surf carnivals" lifeguards challenge each other in skills competitions.

Ll

M m

When an Aussie meets you the very first time,
he thinks, "I'll bet you'll be a friend of mine."
It's a tried-and-true Australian trait.
So the letter **M** should stand for mate.

The classic greeting in Australia is to say, "G'day, Mate." This is said even to someone you've never met before.

Australian culture includes the idea of *mateship*. It is an unwritten code of conduct stressing friendship and equality. While class is terribly important in many countries around the world, many Australians pride themselves on the idea of a society without classes, without divisions, and mateship is an important part of that notion. Australian lawmakers even considered writing the notion of mateship into the Australian constitution. It's such an important concept in Australian society that some have suggested it become a part of the process in becoming an Australian citizen. The Australian writer C.E.W. Bean summed it up this way in 1924: "*...a man should at all times and at any cost stand by his mate. That was and is the one law which the good Australian must never break. It is bred in the child and stays with him through life.*"

Generally speaking, a man would not call a woman "mate," though she may use the term when addressing a man. But the idea of mateship extends to all Australians.

The story of Ned Kelly has captivated Australians for more than a century. Kelly was a *bushranger*, an outlaw who survived in the bush on the run from lawmen. Born in the 1850s, he was a troubled young man who often clashed with police and spent several years in prison. After killing three policemen, Kelly formed a gang, and together they robbed banks and created a great deal of mayhem. In a showdown with police, despite wearing suits of homemade armor, he and his gang were captured, and Ned Kelly was hanged in 1880 when he was only twenty-five years old.

He wrote a lengthy letter that described the treatment he and his family had endured at the hands of the colonial police. While Kelly had clearly violated many laws, many Australians understood his frustration with the difference between the comfortable lives of wealthy landowners and the hard-scrabble existence of poor settlers who often worked themselves to death. While the letter wasn't published until long after his death, it seemed to shed new light and, for some, a new understanding on the outlaw Ned Kelly.

I'll tell you a tale of a man on the run,
wearing homemade armor, shining in the sun.
An N for Ned Kelly, both hero and knave,
was he cunning and cruel, or noble and brave?

O o

We're hitting the road with a jeep full of gear,
bound for the rugged Australian frontier.
O is for outback where legends abound
and wild and wonderful creatures are found.

Most of Australia is wild, untamed land known as the *outback*. While many of the coastal regions of Australia are lush and fertile, much of the Australian interior is arid, rugged terrain. The harsh extremes of the outback loom large in the Australian imagination, and much of the nation's great folklore centers on stories of squatters and bushrangers who survived the outback through their cunning and courage.

While it isn't always visible, there is a great deal of wildlife in the outback. The heat of day can keep them hidden, but the outback plays host to a huge variety of reptiles, birds, wild camels and horses, and native wild dogs known as dingoes. Dingoes are golden or reddish-brown in color. They eat small animals and reptiles but also eat fruits and plants.

While many assume the outback is an enormous desert, its vast expanse also includes cities like Alice Springs and tropical waterfalls like those in Kakadu National Park. Located in the Northern Territories, Kakadu is popular with tourists for its ancient Aboriginal rock paintings, beautiful waterfalls and gorges, and frequent crocodile sightings.

The lovely city of Perth is one of the most isolated big cities in the world. More than a million people live in Perth, but it is the only large city in the western half of Australia. And to find another city of a million people you have to travel to Adelaide, which is more than a thousand miles away.

Perth sits at the southwest corner of Australia. It's the capital of Western Australia, Australia's largest state.

The city came to be known as "The City of Lights" in 1962 when American astronaut John Glenn became the first man to orbit the earth. When the citizens of Perth realized that Glenn's flight path would take him over southwestern Australia just after midnight, they decided to give the astronaut a show of lights. The lights of businesses and homes blazed through the night. Taxi drivers flashed their headlights. Some homeowners placed white sheets on their lawns to reflect more light into the sky. Sure enough, John Glenn could see the gleaming city of Perth from space. "Thank everyone for turning them on, will you?" he radioed back to earth.

When Glenn returned to space in the space shuttle Discovery in 1998, Perth again lit up the night.

Pp

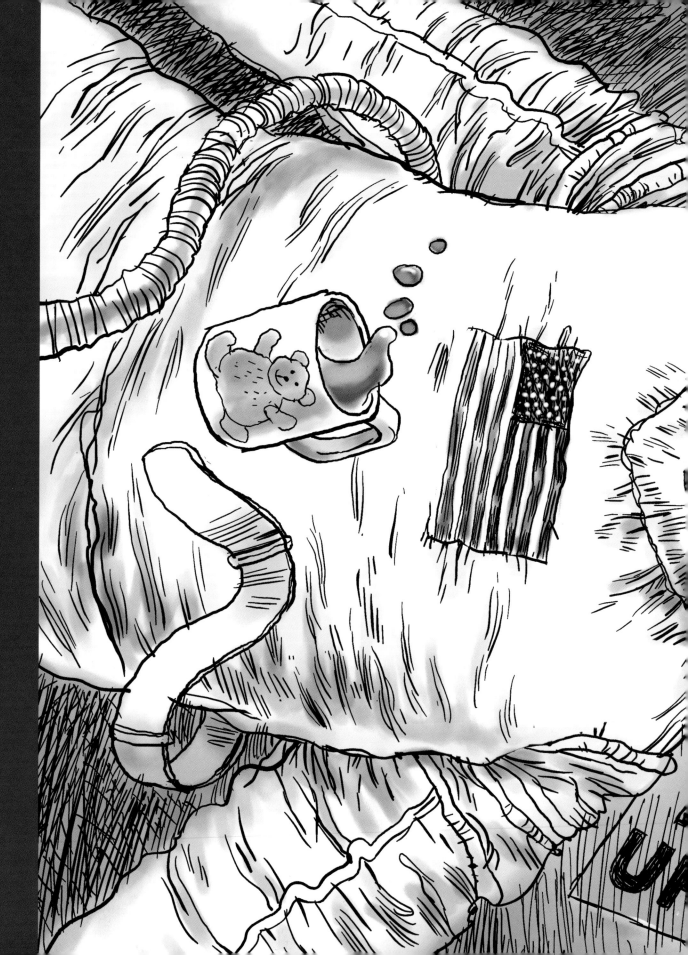

It just may be the edge of the earth,
but way out west, **P** is for Perth.
"The City of Lights" gleams with grace,
shining a beacon for travelers in space.

Because of Australia's location and isolation from the rest of the world, air travel is critical to connecting Australians with other nations. Travelers all over the world have learned to recognize the "flying kangaroo" on the tail of Qantas jetliners. Founded in 1920, Qantas is the world's second oldest continually operating airline. (Only KLM of the Netherlands has been in operation longer.) The airline began with one airplane, which could carry one pilot and two passengers.

Qantas originally stood for "Queensland and Northern Territories Aerial Services." As the airline grew, it became the national airline of Australia.

Q q

Q is for Qantas to help us fly.
The Australian airline takes to the sky.
When people want to see this world of wonder,
Qantas brings them to the land down under.

R r

Aboriginal culture is rich with the stories of the world's creation. The stories handed down through many generations refer to the beginning of the world as the *Dreamtime*. In the Dreamtime, Ancestral Spirits took a gray, lifeless earth and created a world of abundant life.

There are many special figures and symbols in Aboriginal stories, but the most important is the rainbow serpent, who Aboriginals believe gave life to every other living thing. As the enormous rainbow serpent awoke and broke through the earth's crust, his movements formed mountains and valleys, lakes and rivers, and the many and varied formations that make up the Australian continent.

The Aboriginal people of Australia have no written language or alphabet. So the stories of the Dreamtime have been handed down for centuries through stories, songs, dance, and art.

Go back to the beginning for letter **R**, when the world was dark and still.
Back to the Dreamtime when all was quiet and nothing lived until
the rainbow serpent shook off his slumber and slithered across the land,
carving the shapes of Australia, from green forest to desert sand.

The Australian flag flew for the first time in Melbourne in September 1901. The group of five stars on the right half of the flag represents the Southern Cross constellation to signify Australia's position in the Southern Hemisphere. The single Commonwealth star on the lower left symbolizes the unity of Australia's six states and territories.

The Union Jack (the British flag) in the upper left is a reminder of Australia's English heritage. The six states of Australia were British colonies until 1901, when Great Britain combined the six colonies into the Commonwealth of Australia. Australia remained a part of the British Empire for decades, but all formal ties between Britain and Australia were severed by the Australia Act of 1986.

The capital of Australia is Canberra. It was chosen in 1908 as a compromise to settle a long and bitter disagreement over whether Sydney or Melbourne should serve as the capital city.

Along with the Southern Cross, here are some other symbols that Australians hold dear:
  National Colors: Green and Gold
  National Gemstone: Opal
  National Floral Emblem: Golden Wattle
  National Anthem: Advance Australia Fair

A gathering of stars will light our way and guide us right to S.
You'll find them up in the sky, of course, and on our flag, no less.
The Southern Cross is five bright stars Australia holds so dear.
For you'll only see them way down under in the Southern Hemisphere.

We'll take a bouncing ball. We'll take a handy racket.
We'll toss the ball so high, and then we'll really smack it!
A **T** for tennis, for it's a game loved by many here.
And in Melbourne the Australian Open is played each and every year.

The Australian love affair with tennis has lasted more than a century. Records show a tennis tournament was held all the way back in 1880. Australia has produced some of the greatest players in history, like Rod Laver, John Newcombe, Ken Rosewall, Margaret Court Smith, and Evonne Goolagong Cawley. (Evonne Goolagong was an Aboriginal Australian, a member of the Wiradjuri people.) More recent champions include Pat Cash, Patrick Rafter, and Lleyton Hewitt.

The Australian Open was established in 1905. Held each January in the city of Melbourne, it's one of the most important tennis tournaments in the world.

Australians have a love of sports so intense that sport is often jokingly referred to as "Australia's national religion." Along with a national passion for water sports, Australians also enjoy rugby, cricket, horse racing, and Australian-rules football. Also known as *footy*, Australian-rules football was created in 1858 in Victoria. Today it is the most popular spectator sport in Australia.

Uluru (ooo'-la-roo) is also known as *Ayers Rock*. It's one of the most familiar images of the Australian landscape. Uluru is an enormous sandstone formation that rises more than a thousand feet high. But as the world's largest single rock, most of its bulk is beneath the ground. It sits very near the center of the country, but the nearest large town (Alice Springs) is nearly 300 miles away.

The Aboriginal people have long believed Uluru to be a very spiritual place, and visitors can see it as quite mystical. For many years, tourists climbed Uluru against the wishes of the Anangu people. The Anangu consider themselves the Aboriginal owners of Uluru and have long urged visitors not to climb their sacred ground. Not only do some see it as disrespectful, it can also be dangerous. Thirty people have died climbing the steep and often slippery surface of Uluru. And even as it remained legal to climb, more visitors were choosing to admire Uluru from the ground. The Anangu believe the key to visiting Uluru is not in seeing or climbing, but in *listening*, as they believe the area is teeming with spiritual energy.

Depending on the time of day or time of year, Uluru seems to change colors, from copper red to a dull gray.

U u

We've made our way to the letter U,
and it takes us to a spectacular view.
A sandstone mountain, noble and grand,
Uluru stands on a sun-baked land.

For the letter V, take a slice of bread.
Toast it and cover it in your favorite spread.
V It's a national food; it tastes just right.
Down under, **V** is for Vegemite.

Vegemite is a brown sticky paste that Australians (and New Zealanders) love to eat on toast. While British eaters enjoy a similar food called Marmite, Vegemite is a treat that seems lost on most of the world. Thus, Australians and New Zealanders consider it a "national food."

Vegemite is made from yeast extract. It tastes salty and slightly bitter. It's so popular among Australians that it's been mentioned in several songs about Australia, and when Australians are traveling, Vegemite on toast or a sandwich can make them feel right at home.

The most common way of eating Vegemite is to add a thin layer of it to a piece of buttered toast. A Vegemite sandwich generally consists of two slices of buttered toast, Vegemite, a slice of cheese, and lettuce.

Vegemite is made by Kraft Foods, an American food company. It can be purchased in other countries, including the United States, but it remains an obsession only down under.

We'll pick up a guitar and sing a catchy song.
And everyone around us will be singing right along.
Here we'll find our **W**, ringing out before us.
Sing "Waltzing Matilda" and Australia sings the chorus.

"Waltzing Matilda" is Australia's most famous folk song. Those who don't understand Australian slang may be mystified by the story of "Waltzing Matilda," but its catchy tune means that it's sung all over the world (even if the singers don't understand a word of it).

The song tells the story of a hungry but happy wanderer who steals a sheep. He's discovered by the landowner and several lawmen who try to arrest him. But since he would rather die than live in shackles, the wanderer throws himself into a watering hole and drowns. While the song seems to end in sadness, Australians love its theme of living free.

Waltzing Matilda
There was once a jolly swagman,
  camped by a billabong
Under the shade of the coolibah tree.
And he sang as he watched and waited till
  his billy boiled
You'll come a-waltzing Matilda with me.
Down came a jumbuck to drink at the
  billabong.
Up got the swaggie and grabbed him with glee.
And he sang as he stowed that jumbuck in
  his tucker bag
You'll come a-waltzing Matilda with me.
Waltzing Matilda, Waltzing Matilda,
You'll come a-waltzing Matilda with me.

W
W

X

X It's a little risky, our letter X; It just might give you chills.
X stands for X Games, sports with extra thrills.
Hop on a board; hop on a bike; try to climb a wall.
The X Games go beyond the usual bat and ball.

Whether it's a thirst for excitement or just a preference for something different, many young Australians like to take part in extreme sports. These include many of the sports of the X Games like skate- and snowboarding, motocross and BMX biking. But in Australia, there is a wide array of activities that seem *extreme*.

Those seeking extra adventure can go bungee jumping, kite surfing, off-road driving, ballooning, hang gliding, or parasailing.

While we tend to think of warm, sunny days in Australia, snow falls in the Australian Alps and parts of Tasmania. That means Australians can enjoy the thrill of winter sports like snow skiing and snowboarding.

Australia's array of extreme sports makes it a favorite destination for thrill-seeking tourists from all over the world.

Australians have a way with words that is all their own. There's even a slang word for Australian slang—it's called *strine*. And, of course, the Aboriginal peoples of Australia have many languages all their own, and they, too, have influenced many words, phrases, and names in Australia.

Here are a few Australian slang words and their translations:

Barbie – barbecue grill
Billy – teapot
Boomer – large male kangaroo
Fair dinkum – real or genuine
Good onya – good for you!
Mozzie – mosquito
No worries – No problem
Oz – Australia
Sunnies – sunglasses
Yabber – to talk a lot
Yobbo – a rude person

And here's a list of Australian towns and cities that can be real tongue-twisters:

Angurugu
Boroondara
Goonengerry
Indooroopilly
Murwillumbah
Toongabbie
Wollongong
Woolloomooloo

Yy

Y is for yabber, which a yobbo might do.
Do you follow what I'm saying? Do you even have a clue?
To yabber means to talk too much, any Aussie will agree.
If you yabber without manners, a yobbo you might be!

Perhaps it comes from living on a continent so far removed from much of the world's population, or that Australia can be a harsh, punishing place. But Australians feel a great kinship toward each other, especially while visiting other nations. At international sporting events, the Australians can be counted on to be in full voice, dressed in green and gold, and enjoying their common bond as Aussies. One voice or part of the crowd will yell, "Aussie! Aussie! Aussie!" And in quick and throaty response, the crowd will answer, "Oy! Oy! Oy!"

Australians embrace their international reputation as good-natured and friendly people who see a potential friend in everyone they meet. Consider these lyrics to the song "Shelter" written by Australian folksinger Eric Bogle:

To the homeless and the hungry
May we always open doors.
May the restless and the weary
Find safe harbor on our shores.
May she always be our dreamtime place,
Our spirit's glad release.
May she always be our shelter,
May we always live in peace.

There's a zest for living here, and that's our letter **Z**,
for an Aussie lives a life that's full and proud and free.
Wherever you go, you'll hear the pride and zesty Aussie joy.
When you hear "Aussie, Aussie, Aussie!" answer "Oy! Oy! Oy!"

Devin Scillian

Devin Scillian is an award-winning author and Emmy award-winning broadcast journalist. He presently anchors the news for WDIV-TV in Detroit and has been writing as a broadcast journalist since 1984. Devin describes his children's books as "equal parts smiles, sighs, laughs, and goose bumps." His school presentations have inspired countless children to think of themselves as not only readers, but as writers as well.

In addition to *D is for Down Under: An Australia Alphabet*, he is also the author of numerous books for Sleeping Bear Press including the national bestseller *A is for America: An American Alphabet*; *P is for Passport: A World Alphabet*; and *Memoirs of a Goldfish*. Devin lives in Michigan with his wife and four children. Find out more about Devin at www.devinscillian.com.

Geoff Cook

Geoff Cook has been illustrating for 35 years. His career began as a graphic designer, after graduating from Prahran College in Melbourne. Soon realizing he wanted to be an illustrator, he became a partner in the groundbreaking illustration studio All Australian Graffiti and from that wonderful start has been freelancing ever since.

His studio adjoins his home in Caulfield, Victoria, which he shares with his wife Sue, Ollie the dog, and Fred the cat. This is Geoff's first book with Sleeping Bear Press. For more information on Geoff, visit his Web site at www.geoffcook.com.au.